Manipulation Tactics

Manipulation Tactics

How to Improve Your Social Skill and Have a Strong Impact on People.

By Dale Covey

Contents

INFLUENCE PEOPLE

Consistently we are confronted with circumstances in which we should impact, guide, and convince people. From getting your kids to clean their room to getting your boss to give you a raise. It's all about the flu.

Our ability to successfully deal with people determines the quality of our corporate, family, and social life. In the end, our success in life and every endeavor will depend solely on how we influence other people. Our ideas will never see the light of day unless we can convince others because it is such a great idea.

Excellent influencing skills require a healthy combination of interpersonal, communication, presentation, and assertiveness skills. But there is no right way, nor is there a way to influence others. Everything is a factor that affects people.

It is essential to have an adequate understanding of people and their nature if we always want to conquer others in our way of thinking. If you have sufficient knowledge, you can only become a successful person with flu.

The influence is about moving things forward without pushing, forcing, or telling them what to do. It is the ability to do whatever is available to you, both verbal and non-verbal, to achieve the desired effect instead of only letting things happen.

To best influence people, you need to have an understanding of yourself and the effects or effects you have on others. It's about knowing how others perceive you. Sometimes it can be seen as the ability to hone another person. Often you are unconsciously persuaded to see and understand your point of view.

If you can get people to understand your point of view, they are much more willing to meet you at least halfway. Even more, if you make them feel recognized, realized, and appreciated. They can also do something or agree on what they would never have done before because they feel good when they choose.

Here is a top secret for influencing people. Make the other person feel important, and the more they answer you. It is human nature to be recognized and to feel "someone." The recognition was said: "Children cry for this, and adult men die for this."

People will always react negatively to you if you treat them like nobody or talk to them. This ever happens, especially in families.

Parents don't seem to understand why their children don't respect them. Parents often talk to their children, make them smaller, make them feel stupid, and make them feel less important.

People could gain a lot of ground by listening to others first without judgment and criticism, listening to what is important to them, and listening to what will move them. If you know what will move them, you know how to move them because you can tell them what they want to hear. You can easily show them how to get what they want by doing what you want.

Again, our success in life will depend heavily on our influence on other people. So we have to learn all about human nature and acquire great human skills so that we can conquer others in our way of thinking. If you gain an adequate understanding of human nature and improve the capabilities of your employees, you will become a very successful person with influence.

HOW TO INFLUENCE PEOPLE

Highly-paid boring jobs are always available

And the phone never stopped ringing. Every time I put it down, the bell rings again. The variety of people who responded was incredible. There was a knowledgeable young man who had recently left the army, a French sculptor, an actor, and a brilliant student from the University of Oxford. They were the ones I hired. Many others called after the positions had been filled.

What amazed me was that these intelligent and interesting people applied for a job that was frankly described as boring. And although the payment was reasonable, it was not exceptional. Why would anyone do such a job? The answer is that it was acceptable for these people at this particular point in their career.

It is a big deal not to pay attention to the differences between people when you have a lot to do with people in your profession. He is particularly sensitive in customer service or sales. Can you see how easy it is to fall into the trap, apply your standards to other people and, consequently, make wrong assumptions or say things that damage empathy?

It takes a lot of self-confidence to not do it. Because we all tend to believe. The problem is that people have different, often contradictory opinions, but each party is firmly convinced that their ideas are right.

In most cases, don't try to change people's minds. You are unlikely to be successful. What constitutes a person's opinions and opinions is the platform, which is composed of the layers of experience he has had. Since the events and encounters that make up our lives are different, no person can have an identical vision.

To successfully relate to people, focus on understanding how they view things. You can find out by asking right open questions and listening carefully to the answers. This creates empathy, especially when you can make insightful comments that show knowledge and understanding of the other person's situation.

Above all, resist the "ego trap" in which you dominate the conversation and talk about the things that interest you. It can be challenging to be aware of and resist, but it is much more productive to let the other person speak.

HOW TO INFLUENCE PEOPLE WITH WORDS

Managers have used words not only to transform emotions, attract people to their concerns but also to create actions. And actions lead to results

Words are used to show us what our experience is. In this representation, our perception and our feelings change. Keep in mind, if three individuals can have a similar encounter, however one is irate, another is furious, and the third is irate. So the inclination is changed by the interpretation of every individual. Since words are our essential apparatus for understanding or perusing, the way we describe our experience immediately changes the perception that is generated in our nervous system. You and I need to realize that words have a biochemical effect.

The words we add to our experience become our experience. Words have the power to change our feelings by simply selecting different words for the same experience or the same emotions. Positive use of words can significantly increase your ability to communicate with others.

Thusly, we should intentionally pick the words we use to depict passionate states or experiences. Now you have the opportunity to take control. Keep in mind that the words you choose continually shape your destiny. Therefore, replace it with one that allows you.

HOW TO INFLUENCE PEOPLE: A TECHNIQUE THAT APPLIES THE LAW OF ATTRACTION

Today is the day when you have a big meeting, where everyone should be careful and understand where you come from. You need others to concur with you and work in a group. Or maybe you have a colleague you just want to get along with. No, you want to get along, and not just want them to go away. You can do something for any situation that other people are involved in, and it all depends on how you imagine and act.

You can influence the situation by applying the law of attraction and your "inner" self, as long as everyone emits the same type of vibration, and you want to start from there.

Take some time to view it before your big day. Imagine how well the meeting is going, and everyone smiles. They get along and see that everyone is on the same page. Employees who typically have a problem realize they have one of those days when they agree. Watch your meeting the way you want. If it's an employee you want to influence, watch how you get along, and everything happens effortlessly. Feel it, listen to it and watch it in the hour. When you visualize, make sure your mind does not stray, and when you gently bring it back to imagine your needs. When your logical mind intervenes and tells you that this is not possible, gently bring your mind back to the ideal visualization until you feel that it will happen.

Take the time to relax and see yourself at work or where the person you want to influence is located. Start imagining a white glow that comes from within. See how the white glow widens and surrounds the room. Look at the white glow that includes the person you want to influence. See how they feel, how love comes from your light. Yes, love. Love breaks down barriers and inspires others.

When he comes to you, you will surround the person you want to influence with love. If you send love to someone, that love will prevail

By visualizing and radiating love, you are sending a frequency that pulls the feeling back. If the person you want to influence has the same frequency, he or she will be changed. They are affected only when they are ready to listen, see, and hear. They may not have known in the past that this is what they wanted, but if you visualize and reach them, it is very likely that they will start to turn around and see it your way ... if it is in their vibration it is

If they are not to be impacted, there will be no progressions right now, but if they are ready to break down the walls and move to the level of vibration, they will move forward. Remember not to push yourself to influence others. View only from your point of view, not from your point of view. If you press, it will offer resistance, and you will attract resistance. Always display with the result, including ease for you and whoever you view. A person can only be influenced if he is ready to rise or fall on the vibration you send. Extend your visualization with your light, and everything will be as you want!

INFLUENCE PEOPLE AND MAKE FRIENDS - SOME USEFUL TIPS TO GET STARTED

Being able to influence others is a good thing that you can learn to get what you want and be successful in life. Knowing how to influence people and make friends is also an essential aspect of a happy and successful life.

You may think that some have only the ability to earn and gain trust. Therefore, they are often the ones who get what they want in life and make things a little easier for them, whether it's social life, work, or business, even at home. You, too, can improve your ability to influence to facilitate your work and build good relationships.

There may be some complex techniques that influence other people and make friends, but you can start with the simplest and most everyday techniques. Here are some helpful tips and techniques that can help you improve your ability to influence and make more friends.

One of the first things you need to learn to influence people and make friends is to know yourself. Know what you want and what goals you have to influence people and also know your strengths and weaknesses. In this way, you learn to overcome weaknesses and to use your strengths well to influence others.

Be interested. If you want to influence people and make friends, you have to work to take care of them, and you have to be real. You have to know and understand what they need and what they want, and you have to think about satisfying them. You need to take the first step to influence, not just waiting for them to follow you. Many people need and want material things or security, and even if they just need moral support, it's something you can start with to conquer them. Of course, the important things that can motivate people are their needs and desires.

Learn to listen and pay attention to them. Your listening ability is also an important thing that you need to improve to improve your flu skills. If you can learn to listen to people, they would be interested in listening to you. Influencing people is better with good communication, and it is not possible to communicate effectively without listening to them. You have to give people your ears, so they are interested in you.

Avoid common mistakes when dealing with people who might drive them away from you. Learn to practice, not to criticize people. Most of the time, they don't feel respected. Instead of attacking the person's behavior and behavior, criticize the action and help them correct it. Also, avoid too many complaints. This is certainly an attitude that drives people away from you. Give meaning to others. If they believe you are sincere, they will like you even more.

To influence people and make friends, you generally need to start giving others positive energy. Be someone others want to go and be together with. Surely being a positive person is a good way to win people over and a good place to start influencing them.

HOW TO INFLUENCE OTHERS - THE BASIC TECHNIQUES FOR INFLUENCING PEOPLE

We probably all want to learn to influence others. Of course, it would be nice if we could easily convince other people to agree on what we suggest or give in to what we want and make everything much simpler, from your career to business relations.

By learning to influence others, you can also make new friends, build good relationships, and easily achieve your goals and desires in life. To be able to influence and convince, here are some basic things you need to consider.

- Know yourself. You certainly have your weaknesses and your strengths, and it is an important step to know yourself and evaluate what prevents you from being someone who can easily convince or influence others. Most successful people are very knowledgeable, so they can plan well and easily achieve their goals.

- Improve your listening skills. Effective listening is an essential part of effective communication, an important tool for influencing and convincing people. Learn to improve your listening skills by giving people your full attention and sincere interest in their needs. One technique that is often used to influence others is to know their needs and desires and to help them work or satisfy them. Being able to respond to their needs is certainly a way to motivate them to follow them.

- Work to be pleasant. Learning to influence others starts with the people you like. To do this, you must show them your true interest and be someone who gives positive energy to others. Be nice and make people feel important. Learn to care, appreciate and compliment and give them your full attention. If you want to learn how to influence them, you have to give up before you can win.

- Exercise criticism carefully. Another important thing to consider to learn how to influence others and get them to think the way you do is careful criticism. When you criticize, you are influencing others to follow your path or change their beliefs or behaviors. However, it is also very important to criticize correctly without dispelling them. Hurting people is something that can make you unlikely. Do not criticize people, but criticize the action. You could also start criticizing your mistakes before criticizing others and learning to practice constructive criticism. This way, you can influence your thinking without losing repetition.

- Trust and speak confidently. You may not know about the numerous Ummm that you have in your discussions, but these can give the public an indication of uncertainty and doubt. If you let doubts enter your mind, you may also have doubts about following you. Learn to speak clearly and to emanate the trust that leads people to follow and believe.

Start with these fundamentals to figure out how to impact individuals, and you will most likely have a good start in influencing and persuading others to do what you want them to do.

INFLUENCE PEOPLE WITH THESE FIVE SIMPLE STEPS

It is difficult to convince others to see your point of view. Many people are deeply rooted in their beliefs, and nothing that can be said will change their minds.

Sometimes it's not worth trying to change your mind, but sometimes it's very important. There are some straightforward things you can do to impact individuals and how others think.

The following describes the steps that need to be taken to influence people. You can use these steps regardless of what you want to change your mind. These steps may seem simple, but it is this fact that makes them work so well.

Step 1: explain your point of view.

This includes using direct facts and supporting your idea. You should also use an inviting and friendly body language. The main point is to explain everything and allow them to see all the points of view on the subject.

Step 2: listen to your thoughts.

Sometimes you can discover something you don't know about the subject

Don't be condescending or rejecting your ideas. This is the time to build a bridge so they can see your side. You have to see why they feel and how you can change it.

Step 3: Make sure you are also worried enough to change your mind.

Sometimes you may find that you are more passionate about someone else's something. If the other person doesn't care, they aren't ready to change their mind and don't even take the time to listen to you.

You should find someone who cares about what you care about. If you find that they are not 100% interested, you may lose a fight.

Step 4: make sure you show practically how it works.

If you can prove that your path is better, it is much easier to change someone's mind. You need proven evidence that your path is the best. It is difficult to deny facts and evidence.

Step 5: ask them to change their mind.

You have to ask them to come to your side of things. You may also not notice that you worked to change your mind until you ask for it.

These five steps can help you influence others without being intrusive. Most of the time, intrusions ruin any chance of changing someone's mind. You should always be prepared before working to change someone's mind.

HOW TO CONTROL THE MIND - POWERFUL TECHNIQUES FOR INFLUENCING PEOPLE

Knowing how to control thoughts gives you power over yourself, others, and every social situation. You can convince anyone to do what you want, as long as you know how to influence people.

The systems I am going to show you here are both simple to utilize and powerful. You can apply it to any person. Besides, they are safe to use. You can easily apply them to your child if they have problems doing homework or going to school.

Here's how you can control it with a variety of effective methods.

Let the person feel busy with you.

Anyone who has no idea how to worry can use this simple technique. You've probably used it many times without realizing its power. All you have to do is highlight why you deserve to get what you want from that person. You can easily remind an old friend how you helped him in the past. A mother can easily say to her son, "I am your mother, and I have accomplished such a great deal for you. When I do it (whatever you want), I feel happy."

The key to success is to use powerful words like "love" and "happy" in the example above. It is also important to highlight the consequences of the positive result to strengthen the proposal.

Don't give the person a chance to say "no."

This is another really simple method that you can use. One of the most popular examples of its use is to ask someone why they love you instead of asking if they love you.

This is a strong psychological stimulus. Direct the person's mind in the direction you want. He no longer thinks between "yes" or "no." This phase has been skipped automatically. In return, the person is more likely to do what you want.

Another application of these techniques is to ask someone you need a favor, "How can you help me?" Instead of "Can you help me?" Likewise, "What can we do" is more powerful than "Can we do something?"

Now that you know how to take control of this technique, you will surely see how many uses there are in life and how useful it can be to influence someone.

Communicate non-verbally to exercise strong unconscious influence.

This may sound a little strange, but soon you will see that it is really easy. Subconscious communication refers to the use of facial expressions, gestures, tone and other forms of non-verbal communication to convey a message

For example, if you tell someone that you feel good but seem devastated, it is obvious that you are not feeling well. You can easily use this form of communication to influence others.

Perhaps the most effortless ways are to state, "well, I agree" and make a grumpy face. You can start crying easily if you know how to masterfully check.

This is a strong psychological stimulus. Direct the person's mind in the direction you want. He no longer thinks between "yes" or "no." This phase has been skipped automatically. In return, the person is more likely to do what you want.

Another application of these techniques is to ask someone you need a favor, "How can you help me?" Instead of "Can you help me?" Likewise, "What can we do" is more powerful than "Can we do something?"

Now that you know how to take control of this technique, you will surely see how many uses there are in life and how useful it can be to influence someone.

Communicate non-verbally to exercise strong unconscious influence.

This may sound a little strange, but soon you will see that it is really easy. Subconscious communication refers to the use of facial expressions, gestures, tones and other forms of non-verbal communication to convey a message

For example, if you tell someone that you feel good but seem devastated, it is obvious that you are not feeling well. You can easily use this form of communication to influence others.

One of the easiest ways is to say "well, I agree" and make a grumpy face. You can start crying easily if you know how to masterfully check. The effect is similar in both cases. The other person will be shocked and ready to do what you want, or at least ready to negotiate.

The above example is really simple, but you can easily extend it by that. For example, you can easily find someone stupid who refuses to do what you want by saying, "do what you want" and gives them a horrible or mocking smile.

Show the benefits the person gets from what you want.

This is another simple and effective psychological technique. It is usually used in sales, but you can easily apply it to anyone, as long as you know how to control thoughts.

The key to success lies in making the person feel that they want to take these actions and that you are an impartial spectator. Remember to combine these benefits with the person's needs and values.

For example, if you don't want to walk the dog on a rainy morning, you can ask your roommate who has just broken up with his girlfriend to do it by saying that he might meet a wonderful girl who is with his.

EIGHT SECRETS ON HOW TO IMPRESS AND INFLUENCE PEOPLE: HOW MUCH INFLUENCE DO YOU HAVE ON PEOPLE?

How much influence do you have on the people you meet? If you want to meet new people on the net, create new business contacts, or even make new friends, he hopes to make a good impression on them and even influence the way they think, feel and act. To do this, you need to give your new acquaintances the feeling of being understood and appreciated. Here are eight easy ways to help you do this:

1. Call people by name

People like to feel important. When you remember their names, you paid particular attention to recognizing them because you think they are important.

2. Give people your full attention

This makes a person important again. Make good eye contact during conversations and don't let anything distract you from what the person is saying: nobody likes a listener whose eyes wander or who don't seem to be completely interested in what is being said.

3. Seems confident

People can trust - and this is of good quality. It will make people listen to you more and ask you less.

4. Praise and recognize the qualities of people

People like to feel appreciated and appreciated. While it's important not to overdo it or sound dishonest, try to show your appreciation for people's unique qualities and strengths whenever possible.

5. Make people feel needed

People also like to feel powerful. If you approach a person with a need that you have in a sophisticated way, they may not appreciate it. However, if you approach them in such a way as to make them necessary, e.g., "I have a request, and I think you are the best person to help me with it," you may feel more willing to satisfy yours.

6. Know what people need

When you meet new people, try to find out what their needs are or what they can expect to meet you. So try to be someone to help them meet their needs. If you can help other people achieve their goals, they may want to return the favor to you.

7. Take care of people

Make people feel like you're taking care of them for their business needs, or both. It's always nice to meet people who care about the needs of others.

8. Be a good listener

It's not just about giving someone your full attention. If you make sure you understand what people want to tell you, you can appreciate them better because you understand them well. If in doubt, ask questions and show people that you are interested in their thoughts, feelings, and opinions.

GOOD WAYS TO INFLUENCE PEOPLE

We all have our mentors: people who played an important role in one way or another and influenced us in the way we perceive things. Sooner or later in your life, you will likewise find that what you have done or said influences individuals. In both of these cases, you will find that there is an approach to impact individuals, and you will profit by realizing how to utilize this capacity furthering your potential benefit.

There is a very set in a stone manner to impact individuals. The most significant thing when attempting to impact individuals is that you get a positive outcome. Your prosperity as a pioneer or part of a gathering, and in life in general, depends on your ability to influence people and positively influence their lives. Check out the following for a deeper understanding of how you can positively or productively influence people:

1. Send your message.

Take a manager, for example. If an employee is often late for a job under his supervision, how can he convince him to improve his job performance? The first thing the manager has to do is set a good example. If you arrive on time, send a message that you may be the boss, but you are not exempt from the rules of the company, even if you manage to work as easily as you are punctual. In this way, the manager can influence the employee by being a model and setting a good example.

2. If a person behaves inappropriately, investigate the reason for this behavior.

Influencing people in your way of thinking does not - and should not involve manipulation, bullying, punishment, or harassment. There should be the motivation behind this behavior, and if you punish him for the presentation, you will not get the desired results. Find out why. Listen to your problem and let me explain the situation.

3. Explain the results you want to see and get feedback.

For example, if you are a leader in a sales company, everyone has a common goal that you want to achieve as a company. If your employees think they are only there for the money without a deep motivation, you may not be able to make them think that they should work hard enough to profit from the company. Explain the results you want to see to convince them to achieve your goals. The process should not end here, as feedback is also needed to find out if the goals are realistic or if the methods you want to use are feasible.

4. Learn to listen and communicate effectively to positively influence people.

The impact of individuals isn't constrained distinctly to the working environment. Indeed, even as a parent, you can attempt to make your youngsters carry on with the existence they need. As a friend, you are not allowed

You always agree with your friend's actions, but you should always be there for him to support any decision he makes. Listening and learning to communicate effectively can influence others' lives when you have a deeper understanding of what motivates them, which in turn gives you an idea of how to deal with a particular situation.

With that in mind, you can learn how to get positive results by influencing people so you can successfully achieve the goals you've set for yourself and others.

HOW TO POSITIVELY INFLUENCE OTHERS

Influencing people means inducing people to do things of their own free will. People will happily do it for you without fear or pressure. This positive influence will attract people and work with you. A good mix of human skills, communication techniques, and a certain degree of assertiveness is, therefore, necessary to influence the skills. If you have good skills, people will feel comfortable working with you. You won't feel pressured when you work with you. You will feel the need to bring ideas and their efforts to do everything that will make you successful.

One way to get people to feel comfortable with you is not to be too stubborn. Encourage people to express their opinions and ideas. Show them respect by acknowledging their views and ideas. Do not openly contradict them and do not report their mistakes, even if they are wrong. You take it personally, and you won't feel comfortable working with you. Whatever you do, try to find common ground that everyone can agree on.

Always be ready to praise or others when they are doing something good. People like it when they make an effort or help to be recognized or praised. People like it when they make an effort or help to be recognized or praised. By complimenting others, you win them by your side. If you criticize them, they will avoid you.

When communicating with others, make sure the text is pleasant and pleasant. The choice of words is essential to ensure that the message is understood correctly. The tone is as important as it is. Instead of saying that someone is wrong, try to find a middle ground to solve the problem. This saves the other person from embarrassment and does not take things personally when other ideas are better than his.

Assertiveness can make people work for you when you have authority. Assertiveness, however, can be used without commanding. People will feel comfortable working with you. You must be able to present your case to people to convince them. With these qualities, you should be able to influence the people around you and willingly let them work with you.

STEP BY STEP INSTRUCTIONS TO GET INDIVIDUALS TO DO WHAT YOU NEED

Many aspects contribute to a successful business, such as sales, employees, marketing, etc. The key to dominating every aspect is communication. To convince consumers to buy your product, reduce employee turnover, and build good relationships with investors, you can convince them to act in your favor. Let them do what you want.

Here are some tips to help you master your persuasive skills.

What is the most convincing word in the world? It is the word "why." If you unconsciously give a reason for a question, a person is more likely to agree with you.

If you want someone to listen to you, always explain your question or statement. For example, if you ask your creditor for an extended payment period saying "Can I have a payment extension because business is slow and I have to pay my employees," this is more effective than saying "Can I do goods?" pay that they were bought a month later? ".

Do not argue. Nobody wins in an argument. Anger feeds both sides to show that they are right. If both sides are unwilling to compromise, how can a problem be solved?

It is always better to choose your battles. Don't fight for small things, but save all this energy and use it to do something constructive. For example, it would be useless to argue with the bank because they would not grant credit. After all, banks have rules and regulations that they cannot violate. Instead, focus on why your loan has been declined and find suitable ways to fix it

Let someone do what you want by making it look like it's his idea. This was a lesson I learned from Dale Carnegie's book "How to make friends and influence people." It is easier said than done, but once mastered, this can be a very useful tool, especially in sales.

Plant the idea or suggestion of what the person should do. Be as subtle as possible, but keep in mind that this may require some charm and imagination. Create an image using descriptive words so that the consumer or investor can view your proposal, e.g., For example, when trying to sell a wedding dress instead of asking the customer if they want to buy a dress and explain how the dress fits the customer's body type. Create a photo of the perfect wedding day with the client wearing that particular dress. "If you can see it, you will believe it."

Never shout at your subordinates. Screams, never do the job. People make mistakes and learn from them. Rather, speak loudly to express your disappointment as he explains the right way to do the task or face a particular situation.

If you are screamed, switch to defense mode. Anger and fear develop early. Before raising your voice, ask yourself: How can a workforce be productive if you don't want everyone to achieve the same goals? Emotions dominate people. If employees are afraid of you, how can they perform? Will a tense environment make creativity, reason, and initiative flourish?

Never be afraid to say, "I'm sorry." Apologies get respect. This allows people to see that you can take responsibility for your mistakes.

Persuasion can give you an additional advantage in business, which, combined with hard work, can be a recipe for success.

However, remember that a great responsibility is associated with great strength. Continuously utilize your insight to support everybody and not simply yours. Do you get that, Spidey?

The most effective method to get individuals to cooperate

1. Amusingness - If you can make individuals snicker, you will feel better.

2. Grin - The early introduction is the last, and the initial introduction made with a grin is unquestionably a favorable position. Attempt to grin at each individual you meet, and you will comprehend what I mean.

3. Regard - We all realize that regard is earned and not given. In any case, you should reliably respect everyone you meet first. It's always easy to do a favor to someone who shows respect for you.

4. Build an immediate relationship - People who can relate to someone immediately have more friends and can build good relationships than they can't.

5. Use non-verbal communication - Understanding non-verbal communication is a piece of the arrangement. Our daily

communication consists of 55% of body language. Although you unconsciously receive signals from the people you are talking to, knowing how to consciously recognize these signals is an advantage in the art of persuasion.

6. The halo effect - We usually classify people as generally good or generally bad. Any trait you show to someone in the future can be influenced by what you show today. Make sure everyone you meet today feels like you're generally good.

7. Comparability - Birds of a similar plume run together, isn't that right? If you always find a way to find out immediately what is similar between you and the other person, you can easily connect. This bond will eventually turn into trust, which is always what you need to get people to do something for you.

8. Start-up: always be real when you show interest in other people. If you genuinely care about other people, they will become faster like you.

9. Binding: people's names ring like bells in the ears. Call individuals by their names, and they will give more consideration to you.

Mirroring and matching techniques

10. Mirroring Her Language - Mirroring is a technique used in neurolinguistic programming to relate unconsciously to a person. If you use the same language used by the other person, you can set up this report in no time.

11. Regulate breathing: breathing alone can help you build a relationship that you will use for persuasion. The effectiveness of this technique depends on its concealment. Who will ever notice someone trying to copy their breathing pattern?

12. Voice adjustment - Adjusting a person's voice works on an unconscious level, like all the mirroring techniques shown here.

13. Mirror your moods - When a friend of yours is in a bad mood, are you approaching them with a joke? Of course not. Always determine the mood of people before trying to make them do what you want.

14. Adjust your energy level - A person's energy level gives you an indication of how sensitive they are to suggestions. If you can be happy or lively like her, it might be much easier for you to guide her towards your plan.

Apply cognitive dissonance

15. Commitments: If you can get people to commit, they are more likely to do what you asked them to do. They have an unpleasant feeling that lasts for a while when they don't.

16. Utilize composed duties - Written responsibilities are more grounded than verbal understandings. Other than that, it can serve as a kind of contract between you and the other person.

17. Creation of public commitments - Public commitments are even stronger than written commitments. Not only will there be concerns about the relationship, but the person's reputation is also at stake.

18. Use external incentives: business people always set incentives for their employees. Although the motivation it provides lasts only for a short time, it does the job.

19. Always ask "yes": this is a form of conditioning in which the person's response corresponds to the stimulus you are providing, which in this case is your request.

20. Let them make an effort - If you can get people to make an effort, they are more likely to stick to your plans or meet your needs.

21. Generate dissonance and offer a solution - If you are going to make someone feel uncomfortable doing what they want, simply offer a way out.

Create a sense of commitment

22. Give - How do you feel when someone gives you a gift, and you cannot return anything? Pretty terrible, isn't it? You will probably say, "Geez, you have nothing for you.

23. Mutual Grant - There will be times when someone tries to influence your mind when you may feel helpless after realizing that you disagree with what has just happened. Do not worry! What the other person doesn't know is that when it is your turn to get them to accept your request, they are equally vulnerable.

24. Do a favor, take it back. Sometimes people do things for you, whether you like it or not. The problem is that there is a need to reciprocate in the recipient's head. If you are a generous person who

is happy to do others a favor without expecting anything in return, let them know.

25. Sharing secrets - Sharing a secret to create a bond, a sense of commitment, and a sense of trust. Remember, the type of secrets you share should depend on the type of person you share them with.

The power of group thinking

26. Create a group: the bigger the group, the better. People have a strong need to socialize. People bond with groups to have a sense of belonging. If you want people to respect your ideas, strengthen the group, and let it grow.

27. Make Everyone Familiar - If you can convince people to identify strongly with your group, it will be easier to influence their behavior. Also, make sure everyone thinks the same way.

28. Establish Your Principles - Companies generally have principles they encompass in the form of mission statements and mission statements. Employees of the organization or group must learn to adhere to these principles.

The law of scarcity

29. Illustrating possible loss - The possibility of losing someone or something can sometimes make us feel that our freedom is limited. Sometimes people act irrationally when this happens. When you offer a product or service, add a sense of potential loss and see how much difference it makes.

30. Tell them they can't have it - Here and there, you wonder why you're taking a stab at everything to get something you can't have. The opportunity of the decision may have something to do with it.

31. increase demand; Limiting supply - When there is a high demand for a product or service, people flock to it. People always tend to buy what is required.

32. Create appeal - To arouse interest in yourself or what you have, create an appeal by making yourself look special. Surround yourself with good company and unusual objects to attract more people.

33. Show exclusivity - If you try the previous suggestion, you are already making yourself exclusive. People can't reach you and have to overcome obstacles (if you want to call it that). The simple effort to get closer gives you the certainty that they will do everything to please you.

34. Announce deadline - a referral is your biggest enemy. To ensure that requirements or instructions are executed when scheduled, always set a deadline.

35. Limit your freedom - A person's desire always influences his behavior. As soon as you tell people, they can't have something, and they'll want it even more. Trust me, and this trick is a favorite of presidents.

The language of belief

36. Utilize a double language: stay away from hostile words and supplant them with less hostile ones. For instance: use "slow-witted" rather than "bonehead", "correspondence" rather than "promulgation", "heightened cross-examination" rather than "torment, etc.

37. Playing with numbers - When you show something, you play with numbers to convince. Try something like "almost nine out of ten" or "less than five out of every ..."

38. Use positive words: you want people to feel comfortable when they do what you want. Therefore, use positive words when trying to communicate.

39. Packing words with emotions - Emotional words are extremely useful for inducing people to act. 40. Silence - The best thing to do after agreeing is to keep silent. The individual has just settled on his decision, and you would prefer not to destroy everything by inadvertently giving the other individual a logical inconsistency of thoughts.

41. Paint pictures with words - isn't it pleasant to invest some energy strolling around these delightful trees everywhere throughout the recreation center and influencing to and fro in the natural wind current? You can just feel the beams of the morning sun tenderly contacting your delicate skin until unexpectedly; step on a lot of canine droppings. (Enjoy a reprieve. we're not even in the center of the rundown)

42. Pick the correct words - Using the correct words can, in some cases, have a major effect. Rather than saying, "Sir, I'm certain we'll experience difficulty persuading workers regarding your arrangements." Try, "Sir, I'm sure the staff will appreciate it and give you more approval if we try other means."

43. Replace "you" with "let's go" - you can make more people work by replacing "you" with "let's go." The expression "let's go" indicates your commitment. So from now on, let's try using "Let's."

44. Use simple instructions - Provide your instructions in simple, direct, and short instructions.

45. Use everyday language - A complicated language only confuses your audience and / or your readers. Sure, you have a huge vocabulary, but if you always speak like an intellectually qualified person (geek), you are more likely to be misinterpreted.

46. Avoid vulgar and offensive words - Abstain from utilizing obscenities, however much as could reasonably be expected in your announcements (particularly with new colleagues). More often than not, your validity relies upon the kind of words utilized.

47. Stay away from specialized language and specialized language - If the individual you are conversing with works in your equivalent region, this isn't an issue. By and large, be that as it may, you collaborate with various individuals.

48. Shorten sentences - In the early centuries, a single sentence could have been an entire paragraph. Today we live in a world where a single word like "party" is enough to say everything. That said, "let's celebrate."

49. Don't Talk Around the Ball - If you have something to say, say it directly.

50. Use verbs: action words tend to move people. Remember that the words you say were introduced by the person you speak to. Thought precedes movement.

51. Use attention-grabbing words - words like FREE, EARN NOW, EASY, SEXY, and GUARANTEED are just a few of the many attention-grabbing words you can use. Try experimenting with these words by including them in your statements.

52. Emphasize what you won't - see the last sentence above.

53. Time - Studies have shown that speaking faster is more convincing than speaking slowly and monotonously.

54. Avoid voice padding - This means that ... um ... well ... for ... um ... accept your ideas ... um ... don't use these types of words when you speak,

55. Determine the tone: adjusting the tone of the voice by lowering the tone has proven more effective for persuasive speech.

56. Adjust the volume - Always speak so loud that people can hear you. When speaking in front of a crowd, test the sound system first to make sure your audience doesn't become deaf after the presentation.

57. Be clearer: ideas communicated on a regular and consistent basis increase credibility. Individuals are bound to react to your solicitations or instructions if they fully understand what you mean.

58. Take some time to pause - stress doesn't necessarily mean that you should only speak louder, smoother, quieter, and so on. There are times when you need to take a break, so people have time to record what you just said.

Distinction and contrast

59. Triple the value: When you sell a product, people are more likely to buy it when they see the added value. Whatever you sell, try adding a discount, bonus products, guarantee, or something that gives the impression of a good deal.

60. Change Your Perspective - When you talk to a seller, try to see how he divides the price of what he sells into ridiculously small and simple monthly payments. This is called a reformulation.

61. Shift focus - This is a technique that advertisers use to draw your attention to the "lighter" side of the image. Is the glass half-full or half-empty? Is it bad for your wallet or good for your health?

62. The Door in the Face - Make an initially large request that can be rejected. After receiving the response, make another request appropriate to the other person.

63. Comparison of use - Another technique used in advertising. I'm sure you see it a lot on TV. Compare your product or request with something similar but undesirable to convince the person to agree with you.

64. Start at the top with your request - If you ask for a request, try getting a "yes" by starting at the top. Large requests usually get a "no." So be sure to ask for something bigger before arriving at the actual request.

65. Use the right timing - To make the previous technique effective, always indicate your actual request immediately after the previous one.

66. Take note of the situation: are you in the office, in the classroom, at a party, in a church or a bar? Different places have

different moods. Be aware of the situation so that you can match the person's mood.

The power of the proposal

67. Expect to influence - expectation is a self-fulfilling prophecy. Did you know that you can influence people's behavior by showing them your expectations?

68. Consider it done! - You've probably heard it before. However, you shouldn't be the one saying it. When you send instructions, imagine that the other person is saying these words to reinforce the signals of your subconscious.

69. Use persuasive suggestions: doctors are not the only ones who can use the placebo effect. You can use the same principle to get people to do what you want them to do.

70. Emphasize time: what time is it? Well, it's time for you to get people to do what you want, instead of the other way around. Do you understand the point?

71. Use your reputation - Most people identify strongly with their reputation. "Boss, I know you're a generous boy. How about giving me a raise?"

72. Use built-in commands - Here is an example of a built-in command: "You can try it immediately after completing this section. (Built-in command:" Try it immediately ")

73. Peace and leadership: make the person feel comfortable with you, then try to move them in the direction you want.

Involve people

74. Increase your participation: the more involved a person is in what you do, the more likely they are to feel connected to you.

75. Use role-playing games: celebrities often have a hard time leaving their role. Imagining is a simple method to change your convictions. Let individuals claim to open their oblivious.

76. Seek advice - Another approach to get individuals included is to look for guidance. Some will even tell you the best way to do it precisely.

77. Display technology - People who sell cars offer a test ride to a potential buyer. If you can imagine driving a car more clearly, you are certainly more willing to buy.

78. Staying in touch with people - If you own a shop, you are more likely to approach your customers and have a friendly touch than to hang on to your locker.

79. Creating atmosphere - Visual attraction, aroma, and music are used by many types of activities to create an atmosphere and attract more customers.

80. Generate voltage - If there is voltage, there must be a solution. Create excitement like in action in a movie or novel and offer a solution in the end.

81. Enable hands-on experience - Computer software companies release beta versions of their products not only to test them but to convince consumers to purchase the final version.

82. Learn how to deal with objections - let's face it. You won't have the option to persuade individuals to consistently concur with you, but if you know how to handle objections, they won't be able to escape your charm.

83. Tell Fascinating Stories - If you are able to tell interesting stories to your listeners or readers, people are more likely to pay attention and convince you.

84. Use Repeat - Advertisers know that a single ad of their brand on TV is not enough. That's why they continually show the product to bring it deeper into your mind. You should do the same with your ideas. Push it deeper into the thoughts of others.

85. Repack your message: you can use repetitions, but you don't want people to take you or your ideas for granted. Find out how to repackage your message, just like companies repackage their products.

86. Increase tension - isn't it annoying to leave something unfinished? How about if you see this "Continue ..." message on the TV show you're watching? It holds people back for more.

87. Create a competition - To make people loyal to your brand or group, there must be a competition. Create an atmosphere of "them" against "us."

88. Involve the five senses: what penetrates our mind passes through our five senses. If you convince other people, try to

stimulate the five senses as much as possible using the methods mentioned above.

Get people's attention

89. Present new and imaginative thoughts - If you realize how to rehash and repack, now and again, you should offer something new. Today there are a bigger number of decisions than previously. Try not to give it a possibility.

90. Use cites - "The genuine persuaders are our craving, our feelings of trepidation and, most importantly, our vanity. The skilled propagandist moves and trains these inner persuaders".

91. Make shocking statements: just watch the news in the early evening, and you will learn how to do it in no time.

92. Give relevant examples - I think I will leave this alone.

93. Abbreviations and suggestions: people want and need things that make their life easier. We all had this game we call life. Why not share something that benefits everyone?

94. Learn the art of asking: asking is truly an art. Knowing how to use it well can easily penetrate the thoughts of others. Try these interrogation techniques.

95. Let them ask: you are not the only one who should ask questions. If people don't ask, it means they're not interested. Do you have any questions?

How to use flattery

96. Favoritism at its peak - Favoritism in the workplace is highly undesirable. Make all your favorites everywhere, and you're certain to cause them to get things done for you.

97. Challenge the individual's personality - do you have the courage to take a stab at all that you've perused here? Let's see!

98. Don't answer; answer, persuasion is not about you. It's just about your purpose, and your purpose is to influence other people. Failure is sometimes inevitable, but once you have learned your lesson, brush it, and continue.

99. Make them feel important - Strengthening people's self-esteem by feeling important is a very effective technique for convincing. Give them an important stock; They give you a supply of favors.

100. Learn to praise - In addition to feeling important, you must also tell people what you think is beautiful about them.

101. Show Appreciation - Any other person's efforts should be answered with gratitude and appreciation.

Use mapping

102. Use specializations: you don't always have to work alone. Persuasion also includes helping other people. Companies rely on famous people to promote their products. If you know people with a good reputation, find out how to use your relationship with them.

103. Use of the anchor technique - Use the anchor technique to learn how to capture emotions and experiences from events, places, and things in other people's minds. The right kind of stimulus with the right attitude has proven to be an effective persuasion tool.

104. Use signs and symbols: you see them everywhere. Take a look around your room and see how many characters and symbols you

can identify. If you want to take it seriously, you can try studying semiotics.

105. Connect the positive experience: sellers bring their customers to lunch or dinner. Other businessmen do the same. Why? So that they will be remembered. It's like taking your girlfriend on a first date.

106. Use sponsorship - Many organizations support different occasions to make positive affiliations. If you watch sports, look at banners all over the place and try to distinguish which companies represent them.

107. Produce permanent images - Famous people use different types of images to project the properties that people should perceive. Have you ever tried wearing bling?

108. Use colors - There are various implications of hues. If you comprehend what each shading speaks to, you can utilize that information to make a specific state of mind or feeling. When we talk about feelings, we try to understand how to use them.

Use emotions to conquer them

109. Jealousy - Envy is the thing that an individual feels when he sees an absence of value, execution, or material ownership of others. Making others jealous is undesirable, but it is still an effective persuasion technique.

110. Concern - Conviction can be ineffective if the person you want to convince is worried about something. Help the person return to reality by using positive and affirmative words first before using any of the techniques described here.

111. Fear: Fear is often used as a marketing strategy, but you can also convince people by using your words to create fear.

112. Anger - Someone who is angry can be someone who wants attention. You just have to know how to dispel the person's anger when it's time to convince yourself.

113. Sympathy - see that this is widely used on television. Hungry children, tortured animals, victims of war, and so on. If people have sympathy for something, they are all the more ready to help.

114. Desire - Jealousy is the thing that you feel when you see that others have something they shouldn't have. There is a decent possibility that you can persuade somebody envious.

115. Disgrace - When individuals accomplish something they lament, they might be roused to make up for their slip-ups. If they see any hope left, help them stand up.

116. Compassion - Compassion is what you feel for people who have been treated unfairly or who have experienced unfortunate events in their lives.

Use facts and figures.

117. Cite empirical studies: people are more likely to believe your claim if they back it up with scientific evidence. Sometimes adding the words "Scientific evidence has shown ..." in your words can make a big difference.

118. Collection of witnesses - There is a reason why we look at product reviews, movie reviews, book reviews, etc. The more certificates you can receive, the more attractive your product or complaint will become.

119. Use statistics - diagrams, outlines, factual information, and so forth. All of these numbers contain numbers that you can use to provide better evidence to your listeners or readers.

120. Create an analogy: Sometimes, you can explain something for a long time, but people may still not understand it. Using analogies is like making people watch a theatrical version of a novel.

121. View published reports: if they are documented or published in a newspaper, you can use them to support your complaint.

HOW TO INFLUENCE IN STYLE

The desire to influence other people is a natural part of being human. The way it influences - your style - has been determined by your experience and learning over the years. You have unconsciously discovered what worked for you. However, everyone is different, and people will have found alternative ways of influencing. Psychology suggests that when it comes to being influenced, one is more accessible when the other person uses their favorite style.

As a result, you need to learn how to adapt your style to other people if you want to be more successful. This requires that you watch carefully how you work. There is a wide range of viewpoints to consider, and we have made a far-reaching educational plan to build up individuals' impact and political skills. A key element here is to set your favorite style and then learn to become more flexible.

Via delle natures

With years of life experience, you have created a preferred way of working. From the schoolyard to the workplace, you've perfected your natural way of getting what you want. Maybe you've learned something about the value of integrity along the way, and maybe you've taken some courses to improve your skills. All this learning gives you our seemingly natural way of influencing.

A colleague and I have managed to reduce this to four different style dimensions, which must be taken into consideration when evaluating one's approach to the flu. This is not all that is required, but I have seen some noticeable changes in people who have managed to understand exactly where they are in these dimensions and have started to think differently about how they interact with others to convince and exercise influence. The key dimensions are

Touch and diplomacy

Determination and domination

Gravitas and emotional management

Sociability and networking

How do they accumulate in these areas? Have managed to develop a wonderful balance between these four dimensions. The behavior behind each of these elements seems natural, and they can adapt their style to the situation and the people they are dealing with. In one day, they can be extremely determined and energetic while having a big happy smile on their faces. On other days, they look very serious; they stand up and hold the cards close to their chests. Whatever style you need, they fit naturally.

Maintain your style of influence

How do you plan to measure yourself based on your initial perception of these dimensions? Where do you think you are on these stairs? What do you think you should work to achieve a better balance? Develop the following questions to develop yourself.

First of all, answer the following questions for each dimension ...

When was I exceptionally good at this?

Um ... isn't it okay?

Who is a good model for this?

What exactly are you doing in this regard?

What prevents me from being more like this?

How could I do it

Now you have thought about the size. Let's think about the changes.

In the past week, list three things (for each size) that you could have done differently.

What would have been the disadvantage if I had done these things?

What about the advantage of everyone?

Could you imagine it?

Come on - make it possible ...

What / who should you influence in the next week?

What size would get the most potential for each situation?

What answer could you get if you increase the volume in this size?

How will you win if you are successful?

You will, won't you?

HOW TO INFLUENCE OTHERS TO REACH THEIR FULL POTENTIAL

Being an influential leader means that you can allow others to reach their maximum influence. For many managers, this idea leads to mixed results. New managers don't want to give employees control, and insecure managers fear that a team member will surpass them in terms of knowledge and skills. Key managers take on the weight of every decision and action until they run out. Influential leaders realize that leadership is not a position, but a well-deserved title that is given only to those who guide through the splendor and strengths of their people.

The Leadership Pipeline book describes the growth process for new managers. Many leaders believe that when promoted, they receive greater powers and freedoms. The opposite is true, a title does not allow people to follow, and without good leadership skills, it can be difficult to climb a hill like a rock.

Managers who choose to become a person who wants to follow others find leadership much easier. It is based on a distributed work environment, responsibility, and collaboration. Do you think of a mentor or a coach you once had, have they guided you with authority or encouraged you, watched you grow and inspired you to do your best?

The best blessing that a director can offer to himself and his employees is to give them the strength to stretch and grow and to reach their full potential, even if it means exceeding that of their leader. How can you empower others to reach their full potential?

1. Know your employees, know their basic knowledge, skills and abilities, strengths, and desires.

Not all employees will reflect on your talents and abilities, but they will recognize the talents and strengths they have to offer and think about how they can use them to maximize their potential. Identify gaps in your personal and professional development and work together to develop a plan to fill these gaps. Look at the gaps you've identified. Are they gaps in your employees' skills, or have you identified a gap that only shows the difference between yours and theirs?

Remember that you were promoted to manager, but it wasn't. It is, therefore, not uncommon for your employees not to have the same skills as before you were promoted. Instead, identify what skills, abilities, and knowledge are needed to do your job well (and feel personally satisfied) and develop those skills and abilities. Also, keep in mind that if you develop your employees and are one step away from learning the latest technologies, your employees may exceed your skills. Don't let yourself be threatened, but be proud to help them succeed.

2. Know that it is your job to empower your employees.

Is an employee's performance inadequate? How do you react as a manager? Do you feel ready to fire an employee, or are you tired of the lack of compliance? As an influential manager, you also take care of the well-being of the organization you serve. Did you know that the cost of hiring and training a new employee far exceeds the cost and time of offering to change the performance of an existing team member? Can you afford it in today's economy? Remember why you took the lead in the first place to achieve success in the organization through the work of your employees. If someone does not appear, do not put them further on the ground by complaining or threatening to fire them. Anxiety and negativity never accumulate well. Instead, focus on what works well and let them use their strengths as they learn to change the skills required for excellence. Reward them for positive action and let them know that you are helping them learn. Most parents would not raise their children to adulthood if they had the opportunity to refuse them for bad behavior at any time. You would engage yourself in the role of leader, as you would do with a parent with patient guidance, affirming the direction with positive consideration.

3. Authorize your team members in their one

Most employees interact with customers in some way. Many are successful because of their integrity, others because of their ability to strengthen relationships, others because of their technical expertise. You want your customers to be satisfied. What does it matter? Enjoy the uniqueness of your employees and the gifts they have to offer. Recognize them in front of others. Model recognition and praise so that your team members can use this ability with others. Inspired enthusiasm is contagious and spreads like a virus from one employee to another, as well as to your customers and the industry. Let your team members know they work for a company that allows them to be authentic.

4. Model as a cheerleader.

Become a cheerleader and achieve your success through praise and verbal recognition. Yes, when it comes to it, we are as simple as Pavlov's dogs, we will always work for the price.

Without permission to succeed in their way, and without recognition, you will simply deprive your team members of the excitement, commitment, and joy that make your job more difficult. Isn't it easier to quickly praise than to pass one meeting after another and try to act as an executor and then fire an employee you've changed for months? What happens to the morals of others? An entire team can be overthrown by the lack of support from one of its team members. When you help one employee succeed, other team members also imitate that behavior and work together to support the other's success.

5. Turn over, authority staff.

Management expert Peter Drucker said: "No manager ever suffered because his subordinates were strong and effective." People become strong when they can make decisions, act, and solve problems. The Boeing 777 was developed with 2000 Boeing employees sitting in an aircraft holder and asked what the company should do next. Teams work best together when they are able to decide what good performance is and identify specific goals, measures, and measures to help them achieve success. Treat your team members as adults and use their collective intelligence to make the decisions that best suit the interests of the organization. Simplify your life. Leadership does not mean that you have to manage everything, hand over the staff of authority, and see how magic occurs.

6. Let others drive.

Leadership is not a title or a place to sit. Guided tours take place at all levels. Employee engagement increases dramatically when employees are allowed to drive on the spot. Do you have a team member who has a little more opinion than others who can somehow quickly and easily win the remaining team's alliance? Do you have the feeling that a mutiny might occur, and do you want this person to sit down quickly and listen to your authority? Use this leader's skills to delegate, challenge, and motivate your team. Managers are seething from all areas, allowing them to drive from their position, and not only will their performance excel, but they will also have a positive impact on the following.

A position is not a leader, and if people follow because they want to follow, it is an influential leader. If you activate these six strategies to strengthen your employees, you will discover that you are a sought-after leader, mentor, and leader who has not only a positive effect on your organization but also has an impact on expanding people's lives, confidence, and skills that you serve. Are you not feeling better?

USE CONSISTENCY TO INFLUENCE PEOPLE AND GROW YOUR BUSINESS

Many of your potential customers consider themselves consistent. They like to keep their commitments, or at least think of keeping their commitments. If you want to grow your business, it is always better to find a way to follow what people already want to do than to prevent them from going their way and making them come into yours.

How can you use their consistency orientation to promote your business and invite them to participate in your products, services, and business opportunities?

Here are some ideas to consider.

1. What are your shopping habits?

Find out if he likes to keep up with the Joneses or if they pinch a dime. Your spending habits influence how you perceive your offer. How can you find out? Ask them, ask their friends, pay attention to what they have, what they wear. Do they seem extravagant? Are you worried about how you meet other people? When you start paying attention to people, you have a great idea of what they are automatically set for.

2. What are the values of your group of colleagues?

Which groups do your potential customers meet with? Nowadays, you can find out a lot by looking at someone's Facebook profile and looking for their interests and those of their friends. You might see some similarities that can be used to create marketing materials and presentations so that they can see how working with you will produce the desired results. Connect everything you say with what interests you

3. What is your social status?

Or, more precisely, how do you see your social status? The way you position your product and service appeal to a specific person with a specific social status. Look at the person you want to reach, then look at your marketing material and decide whether to talk to their shortcut buttons.

4. What are your political or religious affiliations?

If your potential customer thinks of a particular way of using your product and service in terms of political or religious affiliation, you will have difficulty making them think differently: don't try. Instead, use words they would use and use terms and phrases that fit their worldview.

5. What are you proud of?

Are you family-oriented? Use it in your marketing.

Is it business or personal success? Use it in your marketing.

Are they goal-oriented? Use terms that feel missionary, which appeal to their meaning and vocation.

There is a wonderful book called "Words That Sell": take it and use it to find words that attract different people and then use them in your marketing to get people to respond.

TIPS TO INFLUENCE PEOPLE WHEN THEY BUY YOUR PRODUCTS)

Perhaps the argument of a pleasant manager for your employees and having a wonderful team under your supervision. In the business world, however, it's not just about personal cards, but also about advertising and sales. Your move should not achieve unaccompanied productivity, but should also achieve profitability. To ensure that your business is combined and achieves stability, you don't have to learn how to activate your employees to be more productive, but how to convince potential customers to receive your products to increase profits. 25 tips persuade people to get their products and become your loyal customers.

1. Target your market

First of all, you have to touch the right people to buy your products. Not only do you close a sales chat with everyone, but identify the right people who make your product truly sophisticated. This saves time and maintenance and hits the center.

2. Sell high-quality products

If you have tortured the feeling of being successful in your sales, you must be successful in your production. You need to make sure that products or facilities can attract customers' attention. You must allow high-quality products that can swell and sell.

3. Set your prices correctly

You need to determine what prices convince your customers to get your products. Prices can strongly influence your customers' buying decisions. Therefore, set product prices very carefully. Must refer to your client.

4. Make your company legal

Follow the laws and find the past part of the rules. If you are not able to upset people to act as soon as you are concerned, you must do it in a way that, roughly speaking, takes steps towards integrity. Register your request and get a license to sell your products.

5. Give samples and giveaways

If you get angry in persuading your customers to try your new products, why not pay the cost of preparing samples or gifts? In the meantime, you may not benefit from it, but it will be helpful to make them loyal. And over time, this will go overboard with sales if your products are pleasant.

6. Return a money-back guarantee

If you offer a guarantee to your customers, show them that you are safe after discontinuing your product or service. It is your trust that gives your customers the confidence to test your products. Simple forgiveness; You will remain true to your words to maintain that trust.

7. Create a Company Website

Build a professional website for your cause problems to showcase your company profile, products, and totaling important recommendations that will create people realize an effect on after trust and confidence, taking into account you. Also, get your hands on final reviews and ratings for your website.

8. Build an Influential Blog

Take the opportunity to touch your current and potential customers online through blogging. Blogging your doer and passion for the issue will have enough money your customers more confidence to realize change following you.

9. Build an Engaging Facebook and Other Social Media Pages

Make pages in different kinds of social media like Facebook, Twitter, and make your business successful and get profit and enjoy your life.

10. Show Your List of Positive Testimonials from Customers

If your website, you can mount in the works a testimonial page which showcase certain testimonials from your satisfied clients.

11. Show That Your Business Is Stable and Profitable

Just after investors, customers have the least trust to get the arrangement of issue, taking into consideration a company that is losing or not financially stable. It makes them think that your needy event condition might compromise your products. Hence, guard your cash flow and sorrow yourself to have an enlarged financial play in operating issues.

12. Get Your Business Certified By Quality Standards

Get your products credited by the International Organization for Standardization (ISO) or the equivalent for your specific industry. If you are providing professional services, acquire yourself or your team credited by a professional board. For example, if you as regards providing accounting services, be a Certified Public Accountant or Chartered Accountant.

13. Build Your Brand

Don't just focus not on the disaffect off from building your business brand, but moreover, pay attention to building your brand. If people know that you are considering reference to an ably-behaved and trusted person, they would, in addition to trust, you affect on. Be a helpful person online and offline. Be a scholastic and an educator. Be a resource speaker or a photograph album author. There are yet many ways regarding speaking how you can construct your brand.

14. Use Your Product

To persuade people to consume your products, you have to take motion them that you are using your products and are glad and satisfy taking into account than them. By using your product, you would be more knowledgeable approximately it and be the best ambassador of your situation.

15. Let Your Personnel Use Your Products

Let your employees enjoy your products. Give them discounts, and if doable, let them have your products for pardon as a privilege for becoming a portion of your matter. Let them become your concrete ambassadors too.

16. Make Your Employees Happy

If your workers are happy and exasperated, there would be well ahead of productivity in your workplace. They would be more inspired to create tall setting products to customers or find the maintenance for high atmosphere services to clients.

17. Provide Extra Free Services

Be generous to your customers. If you lack to shape the purchasing decision of people, you have to create the atmosphere that they are in an advantage. Consumers are not only after the main product, but they are as well as after the subsidiary services they could acquire from paying maintenance for that product.

18. Give people a good mood

Smile, be nice, be available, and be warm for everyone, be they your customers or not. Customers always encourage to inspire a place of influence that always gives them adequate adequacy, makes them feel appreciated, and shows them that they are appreciated.

19. Don't overdo advertising

Avoid megaphone advertising or congenital advertising. There are customers and space that your products could hardly sell, and you are already desperately trying to make a single sale.

20. Be easily accessible

Get a good thematic area or a place where people can always go regularly and profitably to get the job done. Complete your corporate website and social media pages after associations have recommended where they can be reached easily.

21. Be efficient in your customer service

Don't save your customers on hold. Your era and attention are the part of your product that your customers pay for. So behave in a way you can pay, not only for the main product they will buy but also for the time and attention they expect from you.

22. Have timing

Timing is extremely important. So don't try to impact people during the time that doesn't exist to be disturbed. For this reason, you need to know and put aside the personalities, programs, and swing events of your customers.

23. Make personal connections

Also, taking into account the rise of alert technology, the Internet, and social media, don't forget to share and unite the human emotions of your potential and existing customers.

24. Do a good thing

If your customers are committed to being socially responsible and want the world to flourish in a large area, you will be an inspiration for them. You will be inspired to continue your business by sponsoring your brand or products.

25. Amaze your customers

Delight and always agree with your customers; you truly believe and live that your products contain something more beautiful or glamorous. Also, keep in mind that you, your employees, your products, and the price of your products, your region, your marketing, and even your customers, must work together to make people your loyal buyers.

INFLUENCING PEOPLE THROUGH

SELF-ESTEEM LEVELS

Self-esteem is about all the language you use to describe yourself. The way you communicate with yourself can be seen directly in your behavior and social skills. This, in turn, has a huge impact on your ability to influence other people.

Checking your self-esteem is, therefore, crucial to living the life you desire. By building your self-esteem, you can develop a positive concept for yourself to live, be happy, and develop a product lifestyle.

Your parents were probably the first people you looked at as a child to instill your initial self-esteem. Imagine that as a parent, you could strengthen your child's trust from the start. For them, it would be like a gift of happiness for a lifetime.

Wouldn't it be nice if your child had high self-esteem and could act and perform tasks independently of you at a young age? They would become excellent youth decision-makers. Making decisions and having fun is a common feature of highly successful people around the world. It is a skill worth exercising.

But let's turn the situation around. What if your child grows up with a bad self-image? You feel unloved by you as parents. They get used to blaming others instead of taking responsibility. When looking for new role models, they could fall into the wrong crowd and collect bad qualities for someone else. Ultimately, this leads to frustration because they feel misunderstood and have no direction for what they want in life.

Now you can see how communicating with yourself in the way you expect others to do is the best way to influence self-esteem.

Any entrepreneur or entrepreneur, including you, can improve their sales skills and erase the fear of selling forever.

HOW TO INFLUENCE SOMEONE'S MIND BY CONTROLLING HIS ANGER

A person's mind is very vulnerable when he is angry. Anger is a violent and very strong emotion that can trigger many possible actions and consequences. To use the power of mind control, you should know how to control these emotions. By learning how to do it, you can use anger to your advantage and use it as a springboard to guide the decisions and actions that follow.

This can be especially valuable amid contention. You can use people's anger to reverse situations and get a more positive result. Remember that anger is a strong emotion that everyone has. So if you can have control over it, you can be a powerful magnet for mind control over everyone around you. Just be sure to use it for positive results.

Here's how you can gain mind control by controlling someone's anger:

1. What causes problems? The primary activity is to comprehend what is causing the issue. You can't control anger if you don't know

what's causing it. These triggers become your primary tools for what you want to do.

2. Drive anger away from you. Another important thing to watch out for before you start controlling someone's anger is to make sure that the emotions aren't aimed at you. Sometimes this emotion pollutes a person to affect a specific person but also affects others. If you need to be in charge of somebody, the emotion shouldn't identify you as much as possible as a subject.

3. Get the person's trust. Instead of holding yourself back as the recipient of the emotion, you need to convince the person to trust you so that the strong emotion sees you as an ally and not as an enemy. What you can do is agree with what the person is feeling, let him know that you understand what he is feeling and make the person think you are on his side.

Once this happens, it is easier to give simple suggestions to the person on what to do next. When trust is built, the person's emotional state immediately feels and executes the suggestion.

4. Apply anger management techniques. Now that you are an esteemed and reliable ally, you can start using anger management

techniques. One of the most remarkable approaches to fulfill an individual's anger is to send messages subliminally.

The only way to communicate with the subconscious and to replace these thoughts is through subtle anger management.

You can use subliminal messages like:

I am a peacemaker.

I am at peace with myself.

I am at peace with those around me.

I am bigger than my anger.

I am in control of my feelings.

Even when a person's conscious state is able to control anger, angry thoughts - the roots - are in the subconscious. Subliminal anger control is particularly useful because only these messages can penetrate deeply into the person's mind and replace the negative, angry, and hateful thoughts deeply rooted in it.

HOW TO GAIN WEIGHT AND

INFLUENCE PEOPLE

Now, of course, you could try to structure your diet and exercise to have a slim and healthy body, but the obvious problem is that you are getting thin and healthy and frankly nobody wants it.

Good sir, maybe you live eighty or ninety years! And imagine the cost of buying new clothes. Below are a few hints on the best way to remain fat and cheerful.

One caveat: be careful because if you do the opposite, you may lose weight and gain health without knowing what is completely counterproductive.

Eat large meals

First of all, you need to make sure that you eat as soon as possible. You want to make sure you stop your food and wait long enough between meals to be hungry when you sit down to eat. Remember that you want to eat as much food as possible during these meals. So don't stop trying.

Don't have breakfast

What you don't want to do is eat a healthy and hearty breakfast. Studies have more than once demonstrated that individuals who have breakfast, especially high proteins, have more stable blood sugars and eat less during the day. Both are counterproductive. So you should make sure to wait at least until noon to start eating so you can take advantage of the cravings and drop in blood sugar levels.

Don't eat vegetables.

Products of the soil are principally comprised of water and fiber. This means that they occupy the living space of the stomach that you can use for saturated fats and refined sugars. Both are much more important for weight gain: two seats are purchased on the next flight. They taste good, but why take the risk? You are better off removing them completely from your diet.

Don't sleep much

Another thing that can adversely affect weight gain is getting enough sleep. Studies have shown that people who have eight full hours tend to weigh less and have fewer health problems than chronically sleep-deprived people. If you sleep enough, it will only be more difficult to pack extra pounds.

Don't exercise

Finally, make sure you don't exercise too much. This is one of the most difficult tasks since it is quite easy to move without realizing it. If you park a little further away from work or go up the stairs, you will burn valuable calories that are difficult to replace.

You should also avoid lifting weights or doing cardio. Weight training builds muscles, which therefore burns fat and makes you weigh less than when you started. Completely useless for weight gain and cardio is worse because it trains your body to burn fat more efficiently, which is the last thing you want.

SUCCESS: HOW TO BECOME A PERSON WITH INFLUENCE

Becoming an influencer is very different from just knowing how to influence people. At first glance, it may seem the same, but being an influential person has a completely different level. If you are a person with influence, you can influence an entire room by simply entering. As an influential person, you will have people following you. Here are three keys to becoming a person with the flu.

1. Help humanity.

If you look at the influential people of the world today, you will see that they have all contributed significantly to supporting humanity. It is surprising to me that by helping others, you can influence and inspire others to do the same.

2. Be a person of honor and integrity.

Honor and integrity help you earn and maintain your influence. If you have no integrity, you will soon be despised. You will have many ways to sacrifice your honor and integrity, especially when you become more influential. Remember that a scandal is enough to ruin your position of influence.

3. Maintain respect for people.

Don't be proud or arrogant because of the influence you have. If you do, you will soon lose the influence you have. People are attracted to those who respect them. Your position of influence is to help people by respecting them and showing them a way to discover their talents and influences.

HOW YOU CAN SPIRITUALLY INFLUENCE YOUR FRIENDS AND FAMILY

There will always be a mockery and those who like to summarize the reasons why your beliefs are wrong or incorrect. Some of these people may be your friends and family. They may think that you are too religious or too spiritual for your sake, especially if you have just come to the truth and started living under the guidance of God for your life.

Your friends and family may become jealous and jealous of your peace found with God. Your faith in God is spiritual, and this gives you the Spirit of God in you. You must remember that not everyone has experienced the spiritual enlightenment that brought you closer to God.

It is wrong and selfish enough for friends and family to make fun of your beliefs, but what can you do? You can be a good example of what you do with your life. Don't let mockers (society) tell you who you are? Do not pretend to be who you are when you are not because you are not faithful to God.

Sometimes you have to part with your old friends and even your family if they don't accept your beliefs. A man cannot be something for his friends at one time and then go home and be two good shoes for God at another time or vice versa. It is not truly who you are and what intentions God has set for your life.

Most of the time, you can influence your friends and family to better understand and accept your beliefs if you are not fair to them. You are no better than her because you are enlightened with the truth of God. On the contrary, they are naive about the truth of God, and now you can be the light for them to see the truth. This is how God can use you as his messenger.

You can mentally influence your friends and family by leading your daily life. Remember that conversations are always cheap unless you can support them with your actions. If you are a mixture of tricks, say one thing and do another, your friends will not be influenced by an iota. If you preach to them and pretend that you know everything, you won't influence your friends or new ones in this matter.

If you want to influence your friends and family, live a good life every day. Be in tune with your beliefs and the way you live your life. Let them see how your fruits multiply, and your blessings increase by staying true to God.

It also encourages young people to control themselves. Give him an example in everything by doing what is good. Show in your class integrity, seriousness, and solidity of language that cannot be condemned so that those who oppose you are ashamed because they have nothing negative to say about us.